HOW TO

TELL

PEOPLE

THEY'RE

STUPID

BY NOT SAYING THEY ARE

51+ PROVEN WAYS

by Karen Loophollinger

ISBN 979-8877254619

Notice to Readers:

Welcome to the world of humor and satire presented in this book. Before you embark on this journey of laughter and merriment, please take a moment to understand the nature of this content: _Satirical Content_: This book is a work of satire, intended solely for entertainment purposes. It's akin to a literary whoopee cushion, designed to induce laughter and amusement. _Not Professional Advice_: The content herein does not constitute professional advice of any kind, be it medical, therapeutic, or life coaching. It is purely for fun and should not be taken seriously. _Discretion Advised_: If you find the humor or content inappropriate or not to your taste, please exercise your discretion. This book might not be suitable for all audiences. _No Practical Implementation_: The ideas, jokes, and content in this book are not meant to be implemented or acted upon. They are for reading enjoyment only. It's a source of laughter, not a guide for action. _Financial Limitation of Liability_: We, the author(s) and publisher(s) of this book, hold zero financial responsibility for any outcomes, direct or indirect, resulting from the interpretation or use of the contents of this book. This includes any form of financial compensation or reimbursement. _Use at Your Own Risk_: Any attempt to apply or enact scenarios or suggestions from this book is entirely at the reader's risk. The author(s) and publisher(s) assume no responsibility for any consequences that may arise from such actions.

By continuing to read and enjoy this book, you, as the reader, acknowledge and accept this disclaimer, recognizing the book's purpose as a source of humor and acknowledging the financial limitation of liability.

Enjoy the read, but remember – it's meant to tickle your funny bone, not to guide your life decisions.

• 0 •

Welcome, dear readers, to the hallowed halls of corporate wisdom, where the art of subtlety meets the science of the workplace. I'm Karen Loophollinger, your guide through the labyrinthine world of office politics, where saying what you mean is often less important than meaning what you say (but not saying it too directly).

You hold in your hands a tome of unparalleled insight. "How to Tell People They're Stupid by Not Saying They Are" is not just a book; it's a survival kit for navigating the treacherous waters of office banter, a life raft in a sea of corporate speak, and your very own Rosetta Stone for decoding the hieroglyphics of HR-approved communication.

In these pages, you'll find the wisdom of the ages (or at least the wisdom of someone who's spent way too much time in meetings that could have been emails). We'll explore the art of delivering critiques wrapped in a bow of wit, the skill of pointing out the not-so-obvious without pointing a finger, and the finesse of saying "maybe this isn't your strong suit" without ever using those words.

You're about to dive into "How to Tell People They're Stupid by Not Saying They Are," a book that's as far from an HR-approved guidebook as you can get without being written in invisible ink. So buckle up, buttercup! You're about to embark on a journey through the wilds of the workplace, armed with humor, satire, and just a touch of snark. By the end, you'll not only be able to navigate the office jungle with the grace of a panther, but you'll also be the king or queen of the corporate jungle gym, swinging from the vines of verbal gymnastics with the greatest of ease.

After all, in the world of corporate communication, it's not just what you say; it's how you say it without really saying it at all.

And remember, in the immortal words of... well, someone probably immortal: "If you can't say something nice, come sit by me."

Your Guide to the Corporate Jungle,
Karen Loophollinger

buy
it
here

• 1 •

In the symphony of our office's daily operations, where each member's role is crucial, we often encounter unique functionalities.

Among our team, there's a colleague whose approach can be likened to an unconventional device – imaginative yet somewhat impractical.

They present themselves as a reliable resource, akin to a well-intentioned safety feature designed to provide comfort and ease. However, when the alarm bells of urgent matters and critical deadlines ring, their efficacy becomes akin to a gadget that's more novel than practical.

The necessity for immediate action often finds their 'snooze' feature less than ideal.

You're like a snooze button on a smoke alarm

HANDY IN THEORY, BUT NOT QUITE WHAT WE NEED IN AN EMERGENCY.

• 2 •

In the vast ocean of our office, you come across all kinds of ships and submarines, each with their own unique design. Among these, we have a colleague who's like a submarine with screen doors.

On paper, they're full of fantastic, groundbreaking ideas, ones that could revolutionize our way of working. Yet, when it comes to putting these ideas into practice, there's a leak or two in the execution.

It's a case of great ambition, but perhaps not the most water-tight planning, leaving us all a bit submerged in the realm of 'what-could-have-been.

You're like a submarine with screen doors

A FANTASTIC IDEA, BUT MAYBE NOT QUITE WATER-TIGHT IN THE EXECUTION DEPARTMENT.

• 3 •

You know, sometimes in our office jungle, we encounter colleagues who are, let's say, navigationally challenged.

It's like watching someone try to staple jelly to a wall – a lot of effort, but not much sticking. And when it comes to finding their way through a project, well, let's just say their compass isn't exactly pointing north.

They could find a detour in a one-way street and still end up at a dead end. It's like watching a dog chase its tail – dizzying, yet somehow captivating.

YOU'RE LIKE A GPS THAT ONLY TURNS LEFT

YOU'RE ABSOLUTELY AMAZING AT FINDING NEW DIRECTIONS, EVEN WHEN THEY'RE NOT EXACTLY... RIGHT.

• 4 •

In the ever-evolving software of our workplace dynamics, we encounter various updates and upgrades, each bringing their own quirks and features.

Some colleagues are like those software updates that pop up at the most inconvenient times. They come loaded with ideas and suggestions. Yet, somehow, there's always a more pressing task at hand, and their ideas get clicked away with a 'Remind Me Later' promise.

Their contributions end up in the queue of 'we'll get to it eventually,' much like those software updates we all acknowledge but seldom immediately apply.

YOU COULD BE A SOFTWARE UPDATE EVERYBODY POSTPONES YOUR IDEAS

IMPORTANT, SURE, BUT WE'LL GET AROUND TO THEM... EVENTUALLY.

• 5 •

In the bustling office ecosystem, there's always that one colleague who stands out... or rather, fades out when needed most.

They're like a mirage in the desert of daily tasks – captivating, yet elusive. During crunch times, they become the Houdini of the workplace, magically disappearing leaving a trail of unanswered emails and looming deadlines.

Their presence, much like a fleeting shadow, is both mysterious and slightly perplexing.

You remind me of a screen saver

BEAUTIFULLY ANIMATED, BUT NOT ALWAYS THERE WHEN THE WORK'S HAPPENING.

• 6 •

In the vibrant festival of our office dynamics, we're often treated to an array of dazzling performances. Some colleagues are like pyrotechnic displays in the midst of a thick fog.

They burst onto the scene with a bang, radiating energy and enthusiasm that lights up the room. Their ideas rocket skyward, full of color and sound, promising a grand spectacle. Yet, just as we brace for the grand finale, we find ourselves enveloped in the misty veil of ambiguity.

The brilliance is muffled, the impact lost in the haze, leaving us all squinting to see the true effect of their dazzling display.

You're like a firework on a foggy night

LOTS OF NOISE AND
EXCITEMENT, BUT
WE'RE NOT QUITE
SEEING THE IMPACT.

• 7 •

In the eco-conscious world of our office, where sustainability meets innovation, we encounter a variety of bright ideas and energy-efficient strategies.

Among these, some colleagues resemble an invention that's as well-intentioned as it is paradoxical – the solar-powered nightlight.
They embody the spirit of innovation, offering eco-friendly solutions and a flare of creativity that's admirable. Yet, their brilliance often seems to dim just when the night of tight deadlines and urgent projects sets in.

Their light of productivity, though visionary in sunny moments, sometimes leaves us in the dark during those crucial after-hour endeavors.

You're Like a Solar-Powered Nightlight

INNOVATIVE,
ECO-FRIENDLY, BUT
NOT ALWAYS SHINING
WHEN WE NEED IT.

• 8 •

In the diverse circus of our office talent show, we come across all kinds of acts. Some performers are more... let's say, subdued in their intellectual acrobatics.

There's always this one colleague that stands out − not for the scale of their mental fireworks, but for the lack thereof. Let's just say they wouldn't risk setting off even the smallest sparkler.

Yet, what they lack in explosive thinking, they more than make up for with their vibrant personality.

If brains were dynamite, you wouldn't have enough to blow your nose

BUT HEY, WHO NEEDS FIREWORKS WHEN YOU'VE GOT PERSONALITY?

• 9 •

In the diverse blend of our office coffee pot, we've got all sorts of characters. You know, there's one in every crowd – full of zest and zeal, yet somehow not quite hitting the mark.

They're like that big, promising pot of coffee brewed early in the morning, but when you take a sip, you realize it's decaf.

Eager and enthusiastic at first glance, but when it comes down to those marathon brainstorming sessions, the spark just isn't there.

YOU'RE LIKE DECAF COFFEE

FULL OF BEANS BUT NOT QUITE KEEPING US AWAKE DURING THOSE BRAINSTORMING SESSIONS.

• 10 •

In the vast internet of our office life – where everyone's a unique webpage in the grand scheme of the company website – we've got colleagues who are a bit of a mystery.

Picture this: you're browsing through your workday, clicking along, and then bam! You hit a page that just leaves you scratching your head.
These folks, bless their hearts, are like those pesky '404 Error' pages. You know they're part of the website, they've got a URL and everything, but when you try to figure out what they're there for, it's a head-tilting conundrum. They're present in meetings, they're on the email threads, but when it comes to pinpointing their exact contribution? Well, let's just say it's easier to find a needle in a haystack while wearing oven mitts.

You click and click, but the page never loads, leaving you wondering if you've entered the twilight zone of the office network.

YOU'RE THE HUMAN VERSION OF A '404 ERROR'

EVERYONE KNOWS YOU'RE SUPPOSED TO BE HERE, BUT WE'RE NOT ALWAYS SURE WHAT YOU'RE DOING.

• 11 •

In our corporate skyscraper of talent, we encounter a variety of unique minds, each taking us to different levels of thought and creativity.

Among them is someone special, whose mental elevator seems to be on an indefinite pause at the lobby. They bring a perspective that's refreshingly ground level, never bogged down by the complexities that lie above.

It's a charming reminder that sometimes the best views are right where you are, not in the penthouse of high-level thinking.

Your elevator doesn't go all the way to the top floor, does it?

BUT HEY, THAT GROUND FLOOR VIEW IS SOMETHING, RIGHT?

• 12 •

In the leisurely road trip of our office life, we encounter various travelers along the way. Some colleagues are like those serene Sunday drives – easygoing, pleasant, and meandering through the scenic route of thought.

They approach tasks and discussions with a calmness that's as refreshing as a gentle breeze on a lazy afternoon. While they might not be racing towards conclusions or speeding through to-do lists, their journey is always relaxing and full of interesting detours.

Their pace, though unhurried, offers a picturesque view of ideas and insights, albeit taking a bit longer to reach their destination.

YOU'RE THE HUMAN VERSION OF A SUNDAY DRIVE

RELAXING, SCENIC,
NOT THE FASTEST WAY
TO GET TO THE POINT.

• 13 •

In the bustling traffic of our office life, we've all seen colleagues who resemble different types of roads.

There's one, in particular, who stands out as the human embodiment of a roundabout. They approach each task with a whirlwind of energy, spinning through ideas and discussions with a dizzying zeal.

Like a car caught in a never-ending loop, they navigate the workday with a circular logic that's both fascinating and a little bit maddening.

YOU'VE GOT A LOT IN COMMON WITH A ROUNDABOUT

GOING IN CIRCLES, BUT WITH SUCH ENTHUSIASM!

• 14 •

In the intricate jigsaw puzzle of our office dynamics, everyone fits in uniquely.

Some colleagues, however, are like puzzles that came with a few extra pieces – intriguing, complex, and a bit perplexing. They bring ideas to the table that are as captivating as they are confounding, adding layers of complexity to even the simplest tasks.

They often leave us pondering how exactly these additional pieces fit into the larger picture, making the process of finding solutions an adventure in itself.

YOU'RE LIKE A PUZZLE WITH EXTRA PIECES

INTERESTING & COMPLEX
BUT SOMETIMES
THINGS DON'T QUITE FIT.

• 15 •

In the competitive sports arena of our office environment, we've got a variety of players.

Among them is someone who stands out for their unwavering presence, not so much for their achievements. They're like the embodiment of a participation trophy – always in the game, always part of the team, yet somehow never crossing the finish line first.

Their consistent participation is commendable, a testament to the spirit of 'it's not whether you win or lose, it's how you play the game.

You're the human version of a participation trophy

ALWAYS THERE, ALWAYS INVOLVED, NEVER QUITE WINNING.

• 16 •

In the interconnected web of our office network, we all play a part in keeping the flow of communication alive. But there are some colleagues whose connectivity is, shall we say, uniquely temperamental.

They have their moments, brief flashes of brilliance where the connection is strong and ideas flow seamlessly. Yet, more often than not, these moments are fleeting, giving way to periods of radio silence or disrupted communication.

Their input can be as unpredictable as a signal bouncing around concrete walls, leaving us all occasionally refreshing our pages in hopes of a clearer connection.

YOU REMIND ME OF A WIFI SIGNAL IN THE BASEMENT

YOU HAVE YOUR MOMENTS OF CONNECTION, BUT THEY CAN BE A LITTLE... SPOTTY.

• 17 •

In the diverse ecosystem of our workplace, we encounter various species of work habits.

There's one, in particular, that's quite remarkable in their unique approach to tasks. They've elevated procrastination to an art form, turning avoidance into a masterclass of strategic delay.

Their skill in dodging deadlines and sidestepping tasks is not just noteworthy; it borders on inspirational, demonstrating a level of commitment to not committing that's almost awe-inspiring.

you put the

in

procrastination

YOUR ABILITY TO AVOID
WORK IS, FRANKLY,
INSPIRING.

• 18 •

In the diverse climate of our workplace, where ideas often pour down like a refreshing spring shower, we find a wide range of creative ecosystems.

Among them, there are colleagues who stand out for their, well, more arid approach to brainstorming. While others are drenched in the downpour of thoughts and innovations, these individuals maintain a remarkably dry landscape of ideas.

Their minds are not frequently visited by the rain of creativity, yet there's an undeniable allure to their sparse and tranquil thoughtscapes.

If ideas were rain, you'd be a desert

DRY, BUT HEY, DESERTS HAVE THEIR OWN UNIQUE BEAUTY!

• 19 •

In the library of our office personalities, there's always one that's akin to a gripping mystery novel.

This colleague is full of twists and turns, each idea more intriguing than the last. They lead us through complex plots and convoluted narratives, keeping us on the edge of our seats.

But just as we reach the climax, the final revelation, we find the last page missing – leaving us in a suspenseful limbo of unanswered questions and unfulfilled conclusions.

YOU'RE LIKE A MYSTERY NOVEL WITH THE LAST PAGE MISSING

SO INTRIGUING,
YET LEAVING
US ALL WONDERING.

• 20 •

In the fast-paced arena of office Olympics, there are some colleagues who take 'thinking on their feet' to a whole new level.

They dart from task to task with the agility of a cat, yet with the grace of a newborn giraffe. It's like watching a game of musical chairs, where the music is an endless loop of deadlines and meetings.

They're always in motion, a blur of activity, but when it's time to deliver, it's a scramble for that elusive chair of completion.

IF THINKING ON YOUR FEET WAS A SPORT, YOU'D BE PLAYING MUSICAL CHAIRS

ALWAYS MOVING, BUT NOT ALWAYS CATCHING A SEAT WHEN THE MUSIC STOPS.

• 21 •

In the eco-system of our office environment, we've got all sorts of innovative gadgets and gizmos, including some very unique human ones.

There's this one colleague who's like a solar-powered flashlight. They're the epitome of green efficiency, always buzzing with sustainable ideas and eco-friendly solutions.

But when the clouds roll in and we really need that bright beam of problem-solving brilliance, we're often left fumbling in the dark, wondering if the charge will kick in when it matters most.

YOU'RE LIKE A SOLAR-POWERED FLASHLIGHT

SUPER ECO-FRIENDLY, BUT WE'RE NOT ENTIRELY SURE HOW EFFECTIVE WHEN IT REALLY COUNTS.

• 22 •

In the seasonal dynamics of our office, we witness a spectrum of characters as varied as the weather itself.

There's a particular type of colleague who stands out, especially during the metaphorical summers of high-pressure projects and tight deadlines. They start with a flurry of enthusiasm, much like the first snowflakes of winter, full of promise and potential. As the temperature of work demands rises, however, their initial gusto begins to wane.

The resilience and structure, so apparent in cooler times, seem to dissipate under the scorching sun of stress and urgency.

YOU'RE LIKE A SUMMER SNOWMAN

FULL OF POTENTIAL,
BUT MELTING AWAY
WHEN THINGS HEAT UP.

• 23 •

In the grand gallery of our workplace, we often come across some fascinating pieces of... let's call it 'artistic expression'.

Some colleagues are like live-action riddles, speaking in enigmas wrapped in a mystery. They bring a flavor to meetings that's both bewildering and oddly enthralling, turning every brainstorm into a brain teaser.

Their thought process is like a maze without an exit, leaving us scratching our heads in wonder and bewilderment.

YOU'RE LIKE AN ABSTRACT PAINTING IN AN ESCAPE ROOM

FASCINATING, COMPLEX AND LEAVING EVERYONE A BIT PUZZLED.

• 24 •

In the sprawling garden of our office, where diverse talents and personalities bloom, we often find ourselves navigating through fascinating landscapes.

Among these, there's a colleague who embodies the charm and complexity of a well-crafted garden feature. They present themselves with an allure and intricacy that's undeniably captivating, much like the artfully trimmed hedges of an elaborate maze. Navigating through their conversations and ideas is often an enchanting journey, though one where it's remarkably easy to lose one's way.

The twists and turns of their discourse, while beautiful, can sometimes lead us down unexpected paths, requiring careful navigation.

YOU REMIND ME OF A HEDGE MAZE PRETTY TO LOOK AT, BUT EASY TO GET LOST IN

AND LET'S BE HONEST, SOMETIMES WE NEED A MAP TO FOLLOW YOUR TRAIN OF THOUGHT.

• 25 •

In the bustling cityscape of our office, where everyone plays a role in the smooth flow of daily operations, there's a range of intriguing characters.

Among these, one colleague stands out with their unique resemblance to a familiar urban feature. Their presence in the team is like that of a well-placed city fixture, designed to facilitate progress and action. Interactions with them often involve a repeated and earnest effort, akin to a pedestrian repeatedly pressing a button at a busy intersection.

The anticipation of a response builds with each engagement, as we wait to see if our collective efforts will indeed expedite the process.

You're like a crosswalk button

WE PRESS AND PRESS,
BUT WE'RE NOT REALLY
SURE IF YOU'RE MAKING
THINGS HAPPEN FASTER.

• 26 •

In the competitive arena of our office Olympics, where diverse talents and unique skills come to play, we find a variety of standout performers.

Among the team, there are those who excel in an unconventional category, one that isn't recognized in typical corporate games but is nonetheless a notable feat. Their mastery in creating a whirlpool of bewilderment is unmatched, turning everyday interactions into a championship of puzzlement.

Like skilled athletes in a complex sport of misdirection and ambiguity, they navigate through conversations and meetings, leaving a trail of baffled expressions and head-scratching in their wake.

IF CONFUSION WAS AN OLYMPIC SPORT, YOU'D BE OUR MICHAEL PHELPS

GOLD MEDALS
ALL AROUND
FOR YOUR TALENT IN
PERPLEXING EVERYONE!

• 27 •

In the diverse kitchen of our office environment, where a mix of personalities and talents blend together, we encounter a variety of unique contributors.

Among our colleagues, there are those who resemble a particular kitchen appliance, known for its potential to create something fantastic, yet also for its unpredictability. They are brimming with creativity and enthusiasm, much like a gadget designed to mix ingredients into a masterpiece. Their ideas, vibrant and numerous, often burst forth with a vigor and intensity that's both impressive and overwhelming.

Amidst the whirlwind of their creative process, their thoughts and suggestions, while brilliant, can sometimes scatter in every direction, like ingredients from an overzealous culinary device.

You're like a blender without a lid

FULL OF GREAT IDEAS, BUT THEY TEND TO GO ALL OVER THE PLACE.

• 28 •

In the vibrant studio of our office, where every day feels like a scene from a TV show, we encounter a variety of personalities that could light up any screen.

Among our colleagues, there are those who seem to be starring in their own sitcom, effortlessly turning routine meetings into episodes filled with humor and light-heartedness. Their approach to work is sprinkled with a comedic flair, often transforming even the most mundane tasks into scenes of levity and laughter. The seriousness of business seems to take a backseat in their script, as they navigate through their day with a punchline always ready at hand.

Their presence in any room is like tuning into a favorite comedy show, where the storyline is less about the plot and more about the laughs it generates.

YOU COULD BE

A SITCOM FULL

OF LAUGHS

AND

RARELY SERIOUS

WHO NEEDS
A PUNCHLINE WHEN
THE WHOLE MEETING
IS A COMEDY SHOW?

• 29 •

In the enigmatic narrative of our office life, where every day unfolds like a page from a whodunit, we come across colleagues whose contributions are as baffling as they are fascinating.

These individuals, with their unique way of thinking and communicating, often turn ordinary discussions into a complex plot worthy of a detective novel. Their ideas and explanations, shrouded in layers of mystery, have us perpetually on the edge of our seats, trying to piece together the clues. Like characters in a suspenseful story where everyone seems to play a part in the intrigue, their interactions with tasks and projects add layers of complexity and uncertainty.

Their presence brings an element of the unexpected, keeping us all in a perpetual state of curiosity and conjecture.

YOU'RE LIKE A MYSTERY NOVEL IN WHICH EVERYONE DID IT

INTRIGUING, CONFUSING, AND LEAVING US ALL GUESSING AT THE END.

• 30 •

In our office's wild world of problem-solving, where 'thinking outside the box' is the latest corporate mantra, we've got a whole spectrum of creative geniuses. But let me tell you about some colleagues who take this to a whole other level. These folks, bless their hearts, are so far outside the box, they're practically in another dimension.

Their approach to solutions is like trying to solve a Rubik's Cube while blindfolded... underwater... in a shark tank. It's a head-scratching spectacle, watching them navigate the labyrinth of their own thoughts, bypassing the box entirely and heading straight for uncharted territory.

They're the Houdinis of conventional thinking, somehow escaping the confines of logic without leaving a trace.

IF THERE WAS A 'THINKING OUTSIDE THE BOX' CONTEST, YOU WOULDN'T EVEN FIND THE BOX

WHICH IS BOTH BAFFLING AND, SOMEHOW, A LITTLE BIT IMPRESSIVE.

• 31 •

In the episodic saga of our office life, where every day feels like a scene straight out of a daytime soap opera, we've got our share of dramatic personalities.

Now, there are these colleagues – oh, honey, they're like living, breathing TV drama cliffhangers. Every time they're involved in a project, it's like we're building up to this big, dramatic reveal. They start a task with all the fanfare of a season premiere, full of promises and suspense. We're all gathered around, popcorn in hand, waiting for the grand finale. But just as we think we're about to get to the good part, to the heart of the matter – poof! They vanish, leaving more questions than answers, more puzzles than solutions.

It's like they've got a PhD in 'Leaving 'em Wanting More 101'.

YOU'RE THE HUMAN EQUIVALENT OF A 'TO BE CONTINUED...' CLIFFHANGER

JUST WHEN WE THINK WE'VE GOT THE PLOT, YOU LEAVE US HANGING.

• 32 •

In the ever-twisting corridors of our office, where clarity is as sought after as the last donut in the break room, we've got some real characters.

Let's talk about these colleagues who are like those gadgets you find in the back of a junk drawer – specifically, a flashlight. Not just any flashlight, mind you, but one that's been sitting there since the last power outage. They come with all the promise of shedding light on a situation, much like a beacon of hope when the spreadsheets get too dense. We turn to them in our hour of need, expecting that illuminating burst of brilliance. But, bless their hearts, it's like the batteries inside them gave up the ghost right after Y2K. They're there, they're eager, they've got the right shape and size, but when it's time to shine?

Nada. Zip. Zilch. It's like trying to read the fine print in a dark room with a disco ball.

YOU'RE LIKE A FLASHLIGHT WITH DEAD BATTERIES

YOU HAVE THE POTENTIAL TO BRIGHTEN OUR DAY, BUT RIGHT NOW, WE'RE STILL IN THE DARK.

• 33 •

In the bustling stock exchange of our office – where predictability is as rare as a calm day in the stock market – we've got our fair share of wild cards. Let's chat about these colleagues, the ones who would be blue-chip stocks in the Unpredictability Index if there ever was one.

They waltz into meetings like they're spinning a roulette wheel, leaving us all guessing where the ball's going to land. One day, they're brainstorming like they're on the verge of inventing the next sliced bread. The next day? They're as focused as a cat in a yarn store.

It's a rollercoaster with them – one minute we're climbing to new heights of strategic planning, and the next, we're plunging into the depths of 'what-the-heck-are-they-thinking' territory.

IF UNPREDICTABILITY WAS A STOCK, YOU'D BE A MARKET LEADER

ALWAYS KEEPING US
ON OUR TOES
WITH YOUR NEXT MOVE.

• 34 •

In the vast ocean of our office, where navigating through the workday can be as tricky as sailing the high seas, we've got some colleagues who are like human compasses. They start their day setting sail with a map and a plan, or so we think.

But oh, honey, the moment they hit open waters, it's like logic and reason are in a different time zone. They chart a course that's so baffling, it's as if they're using a map of Mars to navigate Earth.

We're all aboard their ship, holding on for dear life, wondering if we'll discover a new continent or end up sailing off the edge of the spreadsheet.

YOU'RE LIKE A COMPASS IN THE BERMUDA TRIANGLE

NAVIGATING IN YOUR OWN UNIQUE DIRECTION, EVEN IF IT'S NOT WHERE WE EXPECTED TO GO.

• 35 •

'In the whimsical playground of our office, where thoughts and ideas float around like bubbles in a summer breeze, we've got a few colleagues who are quite the bubble artists. Their thoughts, oh my, they're not just regular bubbles – they're the acrobats of the bubble world.

Watching them in a meeting is like being at a bubble show. They'll start with a thought as clear as day, then whoosh! It takes a twist, does a flip, and suddenly it's somersaulting through the air. We're all there, mouths agape, trying to follow these aerial acrobatics of the mind. It's mesmerizing, like a daytime soap opera, but trying to grasp the substance of their ideas?

It's like trying to catch those loop-de-looping bubbles with your bare hands – a delightful challenge, but you end up clapping at thin air.

IF THOUGHTS WERE BUBBLES, YOURS WOULD BE DOING LOOP-DE-LOOPS

PRETTY TO WATCH, BUT HARD TO CATCH.

• 36 •

In the mystical fairground of our office, where answers are sought like prizes at a carnival game, we've got some colleagues who are the human embodiment of those quirky fortune-telling toys. Picture a magic 8-ball, but with a desk and a computer.

In meetings, it's like a mystical séance. We gather around, hoping for that nugget of wisdom, that clarifying insight. We pose our questions, waiting with bated breath. Then comes the shake – their moment to deliver. And oh, do they deliver! Out comes an answer, confident and bold. The only catch? It's like they're responding to a question asked in a parallel universe.

The connection to our actual query is as clear as a foggy day in San Francisco.

YOU ARE THE HUMAN EQUIVALENT OF A MAGIC 8-BALL

FULL OF ANSWERS, BUT THEY DON'T ALWAYS RELATE TO THE QUESTIONS.

• 37 •

In the superhero saga of our office – where every day feels like an episode from a comic book series – we've got colleagues who could star in their own superhero show. Imagine this: a character not known for speed or strength, but for the incredible power of digression.

In every meeting, it's like they've donned their cape, ready to rescue us from the mundane. The topic is set, the discussion is underway, and then in swoops our hero! One moment we're talking budget reports, the next we're deep in debate about the best pizza topping. Their superpower isn't flying or invisibility; it's the uncanny ability to leap from one unrelated topic to another, leaving a trail of bewildered faces in their wake.

It's a feat so impressive, you can't help but applaud the agility of their mind.

YOU COULD BE A SUPERHERO NAMED 'CAPTAIN TANGENT'

LEAPING FROM TOPIC TO TOPIC IN A SINGLE BOUND!

• 38 •

In the playground of our office life, where every day is a new game, we've got colleagues who bring a whole new level of excitement to the table. Think of a summer day with kids and backyard toys – that's the kind of energy they bring.

They're like the centerpiece of every office party – unpredictable, always bouncing around from one thing to another. You never know what's going to happen next. One minute they're calmly sitting in a meeting, the next they're off on an adventure, ideas popping like fireworks on the Fourth of July. Their presence in the office is like a surprise around every corner, a splash of color on the canvas of our workday monotony.

You're always on your toes, waiting for that moment when the excitement reaches its peak and – whoosh – there's a burst of something unexpected.

YOU'RE LIKE A WATER BALLOON ON A TRAMPOLINE

FUN & UNPREDICTABLE, BUT BOUND TO MAKE A SPLASH IN THE LEAST EXPECTED WAY.

• 39 •

In the grand library of our office, where every colleague is a different genre of book, we've got a few who are truly one-of-a-kind. Picture this: you're in the mood for a good mystery, something to really get the old noggin jogging.

You pull a book off the shelf – it looks promising, the cover's all intriguing, and the synopsis on the back has you hooked. But here's the kicker: as you start to dive into the plot, ready to unravel the threads of the story, you find that the pages, oh dear, they're all stuck together! These folks, they're full of potential, brimming with plots and twists that could give Agatha Christie a run for her money. But when you try to get to the meat of their ideas, to really sink your teeth into their narrative? It's like trying to read a book with the pages glued shut.

You're left flipping through, catching only glimpses of the story, and boy, does it leave you guessing.

YOU'RE LIKE A MYSTERY NOVEL WITH ALL THE PAGES STUCK TOGETHER

INTRIGUING, BUT MAKING SENSE OF IT IS A WHOLE DIFFERENT STORY.

• 40 •

In the grand athletic event of our office life, where mental gymnastics are as common as coffee breaks, we've got some colleagues who are in a league of their own. Imagine, if you will, an Olympic event for jumping – not over hurdles, but to conclusions.

These folks, they could give any high jumper a run for their money. They approach a situation, any situation, and before you can say 'team building exercise', they've leapt! They soar over facts and logic with the grace of a gazelle, landing firmly on the other side of reason. It's a sight to behold, really. They're up, they're over, and they've reached a conclusion before the rest of us have even started tying our shoelaces.

Their ability to bypass the nitty-gritty and vault straight to the end is nothing short of Olympic-worthy.

IF THERE WAS A
COMPETITION
FOR JUMPING TO
CONCLUSIONS,
YOU'D BE AN
OLYMPIC
HIGH JUMPER
CLEARING
THOSE LOGICAL GAPS
IN A SINGLE BOUND!

• 41 •

In the dramatic serial of our office life, where each project unfolds like an episode in a TV saga, we encounter a range of storytelling styles.

Among these, some colleagues approach project planning as if they're scripting the next thing. Their project plans are not mere documents; they're epic tales, full of twists, turns, and unexpected revelations. Each phase is introduced with the fanfare of a season premiere, promising developments and climactic resolutions. However, much like a daytime drama, the plot seems to thicken endlessly, with new complications and characters introduced in every scene. We're hooked, no doubt, riding the roller coaster of emotional investment, but as the episodes drag on, the yearning for a finale grows.

The storylines twist and turn, leaving us all on the edge of our seats, longing for that satisfying conclusion.

YOUR PROJECT PLAN IS LIKE A SOAP OPERA – DRAMATIC, LONG, AND NEVER QUITE RESOLVED

THE SUSPENSE IS THRILLING, BUT A CONCLUSION WOULD BE NICE.

• 42 •

In the vibrant gallery of our office, where each colleague's communication style is a different genre of art, we've got some who are true masters of abstraction.

Their conversations are like walking through a modern art exhibit – you know there's a deeper meaning there, but it's shrouded in layers of mystique. They approach each topic with a flourish, painting broad strokes that intrigue and perplex. Their emails and presentations, oh they're masterpieces of the abstract – a swirl of colors and shapes where the central theme is just out of grasp.

We all stand back, tilt our heads, squint a bit, trying to discern the core message, but it remains elusive, dancing just beyond the borders of clear understanding.

IF MISSING THE POINT WAS AN ART,

YOU'D BE PICASSO

ABSTRACT, CONFUSING, AND LEAVING US ALL GUESSING.

• 43 •

In the bustling inbox of our office's daily communications, where every message vies for attention, we encounter a variety of unique correspondents. Among these, there are colleagues who remind us of those emails that pop up unexpectedly – the ones we didn't quite sign up for.

In meetings and team discussions, they're there, a consistent presence. They chime in, adding their two cents, much like those unsolicited emails that land in our inbox. While they're always around, contributing in their own special way, the relevance of their input sometimes feels a bit off-target.

It's like opening a message promising life-changing revelations, only to find yet another offer for discount sunglasses.

YOU'RE THE HUMAN VERSION OF A SPAM EMAIL

PRESENT IN THE INBOX, BUT NOT CONTRIBUTING MUCH TO THE CONVERSATION.

• 44 •

In the marathon of our office's daily hustle, where everyone is racing towards deadlines and goals, we come across a variety of paces and styles.

Amidst the sprinters and long-distance runners, there are colleagues who bring a different approach to the race. They're always in motion, back and forth, creating a rhythm that's soothing and consistent. In meetings and on projects, they contribute with a steady, calming presence. Yet, when it comes to advancing towards those finish lines – the completed tasks and achieved objectives – their progress can seem more like a gentle sway than a forward stride.

They're in the race, no doubt, but their method of moving isn't quite cutting the distance.

YOU'RE LIKE A ROCKING CHAIR IN A MARATHON

LOTS OF MOVEMENT,
NO FORWARD PROGRESS.
COMFORTABLE, SURE,
BUT NOT WINNING
ANY RACES.

• 45 •

In the amusement park of our office environment, where each day brings its own set of thrills and spills, we encounter a spectrum of personalities. Among them are colleagues who are akin to a particularly daring amusement park ride.

They're full of energy, always taking us on a wild ride of highs and lows. Their ideas and actions send us looping through twists and turns, each day a thrilling adventure of unpredictability. But just like a roller coaster that's missing those crucial seat belts, their approach to work leaves us gripping the safety bar, exhilarated yet a tad uneasy about the security of the journey.

It's a ride, alright, one that keeps the adrenaline pumping and the heart racing.

YOU'RE LIKE A ROLLER COASTER WITH NO SEAT BELTS

EXCITING AND FULL OF UPS AND DOWNS, BUT NOT EXACTLY WHAT WE'D CALL SECURE.

• 46 •

In the bustling office landscape, where presence and participation are as valuable as a hot cup of coffee on a Monday morning, we come across a variety of commitment levels. Among our colleagues, there's a type who reminds us of a familiar but elusive promise.

They're always up, always suggesting a return to action just around the corner. In meetings and team projects, they assure us of their impending involvement, their imminent contribution. Yet, as time ticks by, we often find ourselves glancing at the metaphorical door, wondering when that promised participation will materialize.

It's a waiting game, filled with anticipation and a touch of curiosity.

YOU'RE THE HUMAN EQUIVALENT OF A 'BE RIGHT BACK' SIGN

ALWAYS PROMISING INVOLVEMENT, BUT WE'RE NOT QUITE SURE WHEN YOU'LL FULLY SHOW UP.

• 47 •

In the wide world of our office Olympics, where staying on track is akin to a high-stakes sport, we witness a variety of athletic feats. Among our colleagues, there are those who have turned the art of diversion into a competitive event.

They enter the arena of a task or a meeting with the focus of a trained athlete. But soon, oh so soon, they veer off course, taking us on a scenic route of tangents and asides. Their skill in navigating away from the main topic is unparalleled, a series of mental gymnastics that leaves us all marveling at their agility in avoiding the finish line.

Like seasoned athletes adept at dodging, weaving, and taking the road less traveled, they navigate the workday with a flair for the unexpected.

IF GETTING SIDETRACKED WAS A SPORT, YOU'D BE IN THE HALL OF FAME

A CHAMPION OF DIVERSIONS AND DETOURS.

• 48 •

In the symphony of our office environment, where every conversation is a note in the daily melody, we have colleagues who add their own unique rhythm. Among these musical virtuosos, there are those who take the art of office chatter to a whole new level.

Their style of communication is freeform, spontaneous, and flowing wherever the mood takes them. In meetings and at the water cooler, their contributions weave through topics with the unpredictable twists and turns of an improvised melody. They dance around the main theme, riffing on a tangent, then another, creating a captivating but often bewildering harmony.

Their words are a cascade of notes, each one an unexpected turn in the office jam session.

IF OFFICE CHATTER WAS MUSIC, YOU'D BE A JAZZ SOLO

FREEFORM,
UNPREDICTABLE,
AND GOING
IN ALL DIRECTIONS.

• 49 •

In the complex machinery of our office workspace, where clarity and direction are more valuable than the office coffee machine, we encounter a range of guides and advisors.

Among these helpful souls, some colleagues resemble a certain type of manual. Their guidance starts off promising – clear, detailed, just what you need to navigate the new software or company policy. But just as you're getting into the groove, following along step by step, you hit a sudden gap. It's like turning the page and finding nothing but blank space. Their initial instructions are spot-on, but then, just when you're looking for the next crucial bit of information, it's as if the manual of their knowledge has skipped a few essential pages.

You're left standing there, half-assembled ideas in hand, wondering how to piece together the rest.

YOU'RE LIKE AN INSTRUCTION MANUAL WITH HALF THE PAGES MISSING

HELPFUL UP TO A POINT, THEN IT'S ANYONE'S GUESS.

• 50 •

In the diverse ecosystem of our office – a veritable zoo of personalities, talents, and quirks – we come across some truly unique specimens.

Among this array of interesting characters, there are colleagues who defy the usual categorization. Their behavior and contributions to team projects are as intriguing as they are enigmatic. Like a rare creature in a zoo that baffles even the most seasoned biologists, they roam the corridors of our workplace, a blend of various traits and habits that leave us all scratching our heads. Are they a visionary or a free spirit? A strategic thinker or just marching to the beat of their own drum?

Their actions and ideas, while always compelling, often leave us in a state of wonder and mild confusion.

IF THE WORKPLACE WAS A ZOO, YOU'D BE THE EXHIBIT WE CAN'T QUITE LABEL

UNIQUE, FASCINATING, BUT LEAVING EVERYONE A TAD PERPLEXED.

• 51 •

In the captivating theater of our office, where every day is a performance of sorts, we have colleagues who are like magicians – masters of the unexpected.

Among these enchanting performers, some remind us of a magic trick that doesn't go quite as planned. They step into the spotlight with a flourish, ready to dazzle with their latest project or idea. As they begin, there's a sense of awe – a hushed anticipation of the grand reveal. But as the act progresses, the rabbit seems to get stuck in the hat, and the disappearing act becomes a bit too literal.

The finale, intended to be a moment of awe and applause, often leaves us all in a state of bemused wonder, turning a spectacle into a head-scratcher.

YOU REMIND ME OF A MAGIC TRICK GONE SLIGHTLY AWRY

FASCINATING, BUT LEAVING EVERYONE A LITTLE CONFUSED ABOUT THE OUTCOME.

• 52 •

In the rhythmic flow of our office's daily challenges, where problem-solving often feels like a choreographed dance, we find a range of styles and steps.

Among our diverse troupe of colleagues, there are those who approach problem-solving with a unique flair. They step onto the floor when a challenge arises, ready to groove and move. But instead of the synchronized steps of a well-rehearsed routine, they break into unpredictable, unorthodox, and completely their own. While the rest of us follow the beat of logic and conventional methods, they dance to an entirely different tune.

Their moves, while creative and full of energy, sometimes fall out of rhythm with the team's collective dance, leaving us all watching in a mix of admiration and perplexity.

IF PROBLEM-SOLVING WAS A DANCE, YOU'D BE FREESTYLING

MOVING TO YOUR OWN RHYTHM, NOT ALWAYS IN SYNC WITH THE MUSIC.

● ● ●

Well, my dear office adventurers, here we are at the end of our journey through the corporate wilderness. As your guide, Karen Loophollinger, I've led you through the thicket of subtleties, the underbrush of understatement, and the savanna of sarcasm. I hope you've enjoyed this expedition as much as I've enjoyed leading it.

As you close this book (or swipe to the home screen, for you modern tech-savvy folks), remember that the workplace is a jungle, and every jungle needs its explorer. Armed with the tools and tricks from "How to Tell People They're Stupid by Not Saying They Are," you're now well-equipped to navigate the treacherous terrains of office politics, the murky waters of managerial speak, and the occasional quicksand of coworker quirks.

Remember, the art of subtly implying the not-so-brilliant light of someone's intellect is a skill, a dance of words where you're the choreographer. Use these lessons wisely and with a touch of compassion. After all, we're all a little clueless sometimes. It's what makes us charming, human, and endlessly entertaining.

As you venture back into the wilds of your daily office life, keep this book in your back pocket. May it serve as a beacon when the corporate seas get choppy, a compass when the path gets murky, and a source of chuckle when the printer jams yet again.

So, go forth, my intrepid office explorers! Be bold, be witty, but above all, be kind. For in the grand tapestry of office life, each thread – no matter how tangled – plays a part in the beautiful madness we call work.

Until we meet again at the water cooler,
Karen Loophollinger
Your Guide to the Corporate Jungle

•–•

Now, let's be real – this book is the perfect gag gift for that special someone who appreciates a good laugh (and maybe needs a hint or two about their own office antics).

buy
it
here

It's stuffed with hilarious content that's sure to bring a chuckle, a guffaw, or at least a snort. Consider it your go-to for parody & prank material, the ideal white elephant gift idea, and just a darn good read.

Made in United States
Troutdale, OR
12/10/2024

26234045R00066